FOR THE RECORD

A COLLECTION OF PREDICTIONS
IN MY INTERPRETATION

JENNIE ORTIZ

I WANT TO DEDICATED THIS BOOK

TO

JESUS CHRIST

MY SPIRIT GUIDES

BLANCA VAZQUEZ

ELLIOTT ORTIZ

DOREN WALES

AND

OMAYRA RODRIGEZ

Contents

Thank you

I want to send a lot of blessings to those people who have had my back and helped me out. Doren Wales, you have been a big supporter in my life, and I thank you for being a good friend. Ferdie Ortiz, I want to say you are the greatest brother anyone could ask for, and thank you for having my back. Marie Ortiz, I want to give you biggest hug. You are the greatest sister in-law any one could have, and I can't thank you enough for all your support. Deanna Ortiz, I love you so much. I can't ask more of you, and I am proud to have you by my side. Thank you. Kristofer Ortiz, I love you, and I want to thank you for all the advice you have given me. Brandon Ortiz, thank you for being funny when I needed a laugh, and thank you for all your support. Miranda Blais, thank you so much for helping me by giving me advice on this book. Omayra Rodriguez thank you for being there for me when I needed someone to talk to and for offering me your support.

The writing of this book would never have happened without the advice and help of all of you. Thank you all and God bless you.

Thank you

I want to send a lot of blessings to Everyone

Aha Moment

Let me start by saying I am putting my reputation on the line by writing this book. However, I know I am doing the right thing. With that said, let me tell you all that I became an Author on October 7, 2016. I am happy to be talking about the book **When the Light Changed Me.** The book began to sell from the start. Now don't get me wrong, it wasn't easy; it was hard work and ten years in the making.

Finally, the book was finished, but it needed to be edited. I began writing my second book while I began the long process of trying to find an editor for my first book. In the beginning, I didn't know that finding an editor would cost me an arm and a leg, as the saying goes. Some people think writing a book is easy. Well, I know firsthand that it is not and getting it edited cost me nine hundred dollars. At the time, I believed the price was cheap compared to the price quoted to me by other editors.

Thinking of becoming a writer, remember that getting your book ready for publication is not cheap, so save your money and do a lot of searching for the right help. I wish you all good luck. I began to correct my second book on my own while I tried to find a different less expensive editor. It was at that point that this book, the one you are about to read, came to life. Let me tell you this book came as a surprise to me. I wrote this book because I had an "AHA" moment. My eyes were opened by a great friend, Omayra Rodrigues.

Let me start the story of this book by going back two or three years ago when my good friend Doren Wales gave me a reading. She told me, "Jennie, you be writing a small book through the years." She kept repeating this. I thought that it was my second book that she was talking about, but my second book had too many pages to be considered a small book. I guess I didn't hear her completely or that I just didn't understand her. Meanwhile, I was working hard trying to find a publisher for my first book, but with no success.

At the time I didn't know that it was up to me, not the publisher, to find an editor. My struggle continued and I did finally find an editor. After the editor had completed his work, I asked him where I could find a publisher. He responded by telling me that a lot of people were doing self-publishing these days.

I was sitting down in a relax position, but with his remark I sat straight up. "Oh really," I said, and thanked him for editing my book. So, I began searching for how self-publish. I found a site, and you know the rest of the story because I published my book. I became the author of my book When the Light Changed me. I was ecstatic that my book was also available on Amazon.

I knew I had to start saving money to hire an editor for my second book, hopefully one that wouldn't cost me over a thousand dollars. I could have gone with the same editor, but I wanted to be sure the price was not going to skyrocket by the time I had finished the book.

In the midst of my struggles to pay bills and save at the same time, something was happening… I began to see the predictions I had written in my first and second book were coming true. I began telling my brother Ferdie and his wife Marie and their kids about some of the predictions that were coming true.

My brother Ferdie and his wife and kids were in their living room when I first began to talk with them about my predictions. "You need to write faster and get your book in stores," they told me.

"If something is happening now and you say you had had a prediction about it beforehand, no one will believe it unless you had put your prediction into writing your prediction at the time you made it. They kept telling me that I needed to write my predictions faster and get my book out.

This same conversation, would go in different forms for over two years.

Months after my initial conversation in my brother's living room, my nephew Kristopher's girlfriend, Miranda Blais, had a conversation with me. "Aunt Jennie you need to write a few of your predictions down and publish them," Miranda said. "For now, forget about the other book, which is just taking too long to finish." Humm.... Miranda was saying the same thing my brother had said: after the event happens that you predicted no one will believe that you actually predicted it unless you had written it down beforehand. These people were all telling me the same thing: my predictions needed to be published quickly.

In my own defense, my spirit guides didn't tell me a day or time when any prediction will happen. I understood everyone's advice, but still I really didn't get it. it was just going over my head, that is until December 1, 2017, that when I had my Aha moment. On that day my friend Omayra ask me for a ride to the supermarket. While driving, we talked about one of my prediction that had come to pass.

We arrived to the supermarket, and I told her I would wait for her in the car. When she came out of the supermarket, she said, "Jennie I was looking at the little books they sell in the supermarket and I was thinking about your predictions," she said. "Why you don't do a small book and write the prediction down and publish it? It doesn't have to be a big book it can be small." I look at her and smiled and said, "Thanks, but I have to think about it." When I drop Omayra off at her house, and I began driving to my brother Ferdie's house. That's when I had my big Aha moment. When I got my brother Ferdie's, he was in the living room with his wife Marie.

I began telling them what Omayra had said, and he looked at me and with a straight face said, "We have been telling you that for the longest time. But I guess it had to be someone else to make you think about it. I laughed and said that my friend Doren had told me the same thing years ago. What I didn't understand for so long, but understand now, is that: I have to write down my predictions before they happen. My second book is done, but it's going to take me a long time to save money to pay for an editor and actually get it published. Maybe with this current book being a little one, I could put it quickly on Amazon or on E-bay.

I went home and began to think about everything including my reputation. Then I remembered, I didn't think about my reputation when I wrote the first book. After all, it was all about my life journey as a medium and how I saw Jesus Christ come to me from the sun. I didn't think about it then or worry that people would call me crazy.

So, I sat down and took a notebook and began to write these pages that you are reading. In this book, I will explain every prediction I have seen in my dreams and I will write what the dreams have told me this far. This book includes the predictions I made in my first and second books.

Taking a leap of faith

My heart is going one hundred miles a minute knowing full well my life is about to be out for the world to read. I know these predictions must be writing down. After that, the world can be the judge.

What I have to say, I say in the name of Jesus Christ and his Angels. I want to thank them for taking me in another yet twist of my life's journey. You never know when Aha moment will happen or where it will lead you. After all, Jesus Christ uses his children to help you change your life.

By the way of introduction also, thank Ferdie, Leah, Kristofer, Deanna, Brandon Ortiz and Miranda Blais for helping me find a title for this book.

Predictions

From my first book "When the Light Changed Me" here are my predictions.

1. October 2002, I went to sleep, and had a dream about my grand Aunt Delia. She was standing in front of her house on her porch. I heard a voice telling me she would be dead in one year. She died on October 25, 2003.

2. The Red Sox will win the World Series four years in a row breaking their record. After the Red Sox won four years in a row, they would win three more times in the years 2018, 2019 and 2020

3. The iconic HOLLYWOOD sign in Los Angeles will fall.

4. An earthquake will hit New Hampshire by the year 2015. Indeed, I have to say I did feel the earthquake when it struck May 24, 2015. I was visiting my Mother when it hit.

5. New York City will be falling apart after being struck by a Tornado sometime by year 2025.

6. Earthquake will strike around the country with such force that we will not know what hit us.

7. If I'm getting this right, there will be two more wars.

8. The economy will hit rock bottom for eight straight years.

9. Fuel prices will go back down from $4.95 after President Bush leaves office.

10. By 2016, a Tsunami will hit the heart of Japan and will shock the nation to the core

I wrote these predictions during the first three years that I was writing my book. Remember it took me ten years to write and finally publish. Now I will record what I heard and saw in my dreams, through the years 2009 until the present.

11. I dreamed about a tornado. I saw a lady run into a closet, and when the tornado struck. I felt as if I was right there with her. Later I learned from a news report that a tornado had touched down in Missouri. The news reported talked to a woman who described in detail running into a closet.

12. I dreamed about another tornado, and in this dream, I saw houses breaking apart like toys. Then I saw every single house in the dream is being rebuilt. This dream was scary, so big and so black. This dream came true when a tornado hit Moore, Oklahoma.

13. I also dreamed about another a tsunami. I saw water enveloping cars, trains and homes. When the tsunami struck Japan, I understood that my dream had come true. I don't know if the train actually vanished as it slipped underwater, but in my dream it did.

14. In 2012, I dreamed about water going inland and flooding people's houses. It looked like a hurricane. I saw destruction and boarded houses. Then I heard a voice saying, "Puerto Rico." This dream occurred in 2012. I told my mother and my friend Edermira Colon about the dream. In December 1, 2017 Edermira reminded me that I had predicted the destruction of Puerto Rico.

15. I had another dream about Puerto Rico. This time I heard the voice say the word earthquake and that it would also hit Santo Domingo. I told my mother about that dream.

A few months after I told her, my mother called me around 7 am. She told me that earthquake had hit Puerto Rico and gone across to Santo Domingo. I call my sister-in-law to let her know, advising her to make sure her parent was okay.

16. In one dream I saw a highway a lot of buildings and cars even a white church, and its steeple had fallen to the ground. in the dream, I felt I was watching everything unfold from inside a car, it was very scary. I could hear the tornado coming, but instead of one tornado I saw two coming from different directions. A day or two later the news reported that such a tornado had touched down in Worcester, Massachusetts. I saw exactly in my dream how it happened. I had seen the two tornados: one in the other side of the bridge and another on the other side of the bridge. On the news they talk to someone that recorded from inside their car. The tornado coming toward them. The way I saw it on the news it was the way I was seeing the tornado from inside someone's car before it actually hit.

The news showed the white church with the steeple torn off. Exactly how I had seen it. That the day I learn something about my dreams. When I dream with open land the location is in the south. If I see building and highways, the location is the city. I see specific images in my dreams, but I don't know when or where a storm or some other catastrophic even will occur.

As I learn to understand my dreams and remember to write them down, I can't help but think about how scary a tornado is, even in a dream, and imagine what it must be like for the people personally involved. I continually pray that everyone involved is safe.

As I continued with my predictions, I had another dream. This one hit hard because I had already experienced a prediction that came true in 2009 and involved family members.

17. That night, I went to bed and began to dream. I saw the sky, and the sky began to open like a window. Then a group of ladies began to scream saying, **"Come it is time to come home! Let's go; it's time for you to come home!"** It was strange dream, but I knew it was family members who were saying, **"Let's go! It's time to come home!"**

They were around six women in total in the window. Months went by. It was summer, and I was driving my mother Nellie to the store when she told me our cousin Nelson was sick. I look at her and said, "Mom, I need to tell you something, and I hope I am wrong, but he's not going to make it. On July 9, 2010, Nelson lost his battle with colon cancer

18. I can't tell you how many times I told My Aunt Maria and Uncle Edward predictions that have always come true. My Aunt Maria moved from Florida in the summer of 2007 while I was going through my spiritual awakening. She came to stay at my mother Nellie's house to wait for my uncle who was finishing up his job in Florida. They moved next door from my mother house. I said to my aunt and uncle, "Don't unpack because you be moving soon." Well, sure enough, they moved seven months later. Again, I told her, "Don't unpack. You will be moving again." No lie... Six months went by and they moved again. This time, she said to me, "I love this place and I plan to stay." I looked at her and said, "No, you are moving again." My aunt looked at me and told me to shut up.

One year later she was packing to move back to Florida. I looked at her and said, "I'll see you soon." I even told her granddaughter, Destiny, "Don't unpack. You guys will be back soon." Well, I have to say Destiny moved back to New Hampshire, and my Aunt and Uncle are planning to move back as well.

If they move again, I let you all know. (joke ha ha) I guess I am on a roll with my Aunt Maria and Uncle Edward. They should listen to me by now and just don't unpack.

19 This one surprised me December 1, 2012 I was at my mother's house. She was watching the Spanish channel on TV, and at the time Jenni Rivera, the singer, was on. My mother said, "I love her songs." While we were watching and listening to her sing, I heard my spirit guide say to me that Jenni River will die in an airplane crash.

I was in shock. But I didn't worry because I thought this will probably happen when she's older. I never asked my spirit guide when it would happen. I left my mother house a few minutes later after. Almost a week went by when I got a text from my sister in-law Yamir. The text only said Jenni Rivera is dead.

I decided to call Yamir to ask her again who she was talking about. She said the Mexican singer Jenni Rivera is dead, and I asked how she died. "In an airplane crash," she said. I felt my body get cold. I hand up, and quickly called my mother Nellie and asked her if she was watching TV. "No, she said." I said, mom "Jenni Rivera is dead." She screamed saying, "No, it can't be." My aunt Maria was over and asked what was going on. I heard my mom crying as she told my aunt about Jenni Rivera. I did tell my mom about my prediction, but I never thought that a week later Jenni Rivera would actually be gone.

I will tell you a few predictions that I wrote in my second book and let you be the judge.

1. By 2018, and beyond three tsunamis will hit the coast of the northeastern Japan. will wake up the, world for six times.

2. A massive tornado will hit the middle of the United States and travel as far as New Jersey. There will be devastation everywhere.

3. This prediction is not good for animal lover's animal will die from a blood disease that in turn kills some dogs, cats, and horses. But a vaccine will be discovered in a nick of time.

4. The economy will improve a little

5. The United States will fall with such force that the economy will not recover until 2018 and 2019.

6. The air force will experience one of the biggest scandals we've ever seen, but in time it will recover.

7. We will see a downfall of many big name's stores.

8. We all will see more famous of movie stars that we have all grown to love as well as movie producers fall from grace as a result of sex scandals.

9. Most banks in America will fail by year 2029. But, not, all banks, will close.

10. We need to keep an eye on the third or fourth president after Obama, because he or she will, not help anyone out.

11. Foreclosure of all the houses will continue to fall for the next 10 to 15 years, but the economy will not come back fast. For those who have lost their houses, don't you worry, you will come back to own one again?

And 40% of Americans will be heartbroken because all won't see a job for a long-time. Other will be homeless. And almost all United States companies will not have insurance for everyone.

12. Earthquakes will raise to a 10.7 and it can hit the coast of the Middle East between 2018 and 2019. Watch out for the third earthquake in addition to four or five smaller ones.

13. Life won't come easy. But the United States needs to be very prepared for what is coming, and the country will no longer be free. America the way of life will go backward. Yes, life will go backwards because hate crimes will rise between Latinos themselves.

14. Life will not be easy for different states within the United States. Crime against immigrants will raise. But not all immigrants are Mexican. There are other people from different countries like Canada.

15. Yes, people will experience horror when a hate crime happens to a 10-year-old kid. The entire world will be very sad, but the experience will open people's eyes.

16. Schools around the country cut sports programs for everyone. This will be a terrible loss for skilled and talented children. This will happen because grown-ups will lose sight of kids as being innocent and instead focus on other things.

17. The salvation of the human spirits changed one more time for those looking for salvation they will think the world might end and the world will not end.

18. Immigration laws will change between 2013 and 2014, and people will no longer be treated like criminals for just trying to better their lives.

19. Nothing but humiliation will hit the White House because it will be money stolen. People will see the light soon enough.

20. The United States will abolish the right to vote.

These are the predictions I been told or have seen in my dreams. Now, I will sit down and let my spirit guides tell me more predictions.

New predictions

On December 13, 2017 I sat down and asked in the name of the Holy Spirit that all my angles would guide me in the loyalty the word of God.

I am ready to receive the messages from my spirit guides Theresa, John, and Lynn. I let my hands and my heart do the work for them. First, I will let you know how I got to know all three spirit Guides. These guides been with me from the start. When I began to hear them, for the first time was when they were arguing among themselves about who would speak to me first.

This happened when I went on a vacation to Virginia with my mother Nellie, my brother Ferdie and his wife and their kids in a RV. I went back to sleep for the second time after asking my mother for a cup of water. I thought had been sleeping for a long time when I heard people arguing. I assumed what I heard was people outside or next to the motor home.

I thought I was screaming in real life, and screamed, "Shut up" and they got quiet. I saw them when they turn toward me. I could not see their faces at the time, but when John spoke to me, I got scared and began to pray calling out Jesus Christ to help me.

Now I don't really understand why I didn't let John speak, but for some reason I became calm and let my two other spirit guides, Theresa and Lynn, speak to me. They told me their names and where they came from and what year they were born.

When I woke up and the first thing, I saw was a worm hole closing. I got scared, called out to my mother Nellie, and told her that they had spoken to me. My mother said, "How that impossible? You just put your head back down after I gave you the cup of water." I know now that I was hearing and seeing the worm hole for the first time and that I could not explain what I saw. The next day my brother Ferdie found me sleeping with the kids.

While writing this down I had back flashes remembering that night. I just remember I thought I was looking out a window thinking I was screaming at them. In reality, they were in front of me. They turned toward me spoke to me that night

Now I let these three spirit guides tell me predictions and what ever else they need to tell me. I'll let them decide who will go first.

Spirit Guide John

My name is John, and I came to Jennie that first night with the intention of letting her know that God had many predictions for her. Now that she knows that she can breathe easy. Jennie, I am the one that came to you through the wormhole to get you ready for this journey. Sorry if I scare you each time, I come to you. I know you don't like it one bit, but there is more to come, so be very prepared to see a new world from now on. I am here to help you with your biggest journey and that is helping people. I want to thank Jennie for this opportunity to share with her now what I didn't get to share back in the summer of 2001. Now that you know who I am. I am your first spirit guide who wanted to talk to you.

I am here to let you know that the world will change for you and everyone in it. You see, this world is forgetting where everyone came from. I will explain that you were sent here by God. Jesus Christ is his son and the reason God wanted people to believe in Jesus Christ.

Because Jesus will perform a lot of miracles to show and prove to the world, that, he was a prophet of God. Why are the people on Earth taking prayers as an insult and not letting people join together?

By saying this I want you all to know God is big, and Jesus also has his hands full, but together they can make a lot of changes for this world and help it to wake up and unite again. Now please be very patient, and you will find your destiny. Life is about people learning, understanding one another, giving each other a helping hand. Is not hard to understand what God wants. The reason I say that you were born in a body is because everyone forgets the promises you all made before you were born.

Beside it was large reason why Jesus Christ had to get hit with the belt. Because this way people will never forget all the pain he suffered for his people. Let me explain now you know all the suffering you guys go through is to learn from it, experience all the hurt then let it go and give it back Jesus Christ.

All the anger all the hurt he will take, that pain from you so that you don't ever forget that you are not alone. We have your back, and when the end is near, you won't have any regrets. Remember this message is for everyone who is reading this. Don't forget to pray and help who are suffering, and don't forget to pray and let go of your suffering. God has his way of cleaning your sins before your time is up.

This is something you all need to learn about life. Let go of all the drama life gives you only learn from it don't hold on to it. Pray give it back to the Lord because if you hold on to all the anger and hurt you done to yourself and to others.

If you never learn from any of your mistake. Then the promise you did to the Lord to learn from all the drama life has for you. Then life will continue until you learn not to keep the anger inside of you and give it to Jesus Christ and beside your life can become a cycle of life until you learn not to hurt anyone else again. Remember we are all equal no one is different so with that said. I will let Jennie write her thoughts.

My Thoughts

I thought this book would be all about prediction, but what John said made a lot of sense to me. I say that because some people claimed that they get offended by religion. What anyone believes in terms of religion does not hurt anyone else. I have an idea. It all start from the moment we speak to someone like they are not perfect. This hurt people and can make them feel like trash. This kind of behavior needs to stop now. Everything else John said amazed me. I urge the people who are reading my book to think about it.

Let me say it is difficult not to get scared when I hear the wormhole coming. I never understood why I heard it or saw it until now. I don't like the sound of it. Now that I know John, I want to thank him for letting me know why I heard it and see it.

I had been asking for information from metaphysical groups because I wanted answers about why I was seeing a wormhole. I got the answer I needed from John.

Now that I know, I wanted to let you all know my thoughts. I decided to let other two spirit guides tell me more.

Spirit Guide Lynn

Hi Jennie, I am here to guide you through the toughest challenges in the world. I have to tell you about some big challenges the world will face through the years. Here are a few.

1. People and you need to know now that hard times are coming and a lot people will be suffering from world destructions. Tornado will hit so many places that there be no way people can help each other. Why do I say that so much destruction in the universe can help by bringing a lot of you home? having made this negative statement, let me explain it. The world will see tornado will hit seven cities so hard that not a single person on Earth will try to help because they just can't. The destruction will hit at the same time, and no one will know who or how to help. The damage will simply be too great and widespread. There won't be enough people to volunteer to help.

2. Now I'll give you a clue. By 2026 there be a hurricane that will destroy another island again, and this time it will be even worse than the first two times.

3. The humans will see miracles after miracles and those that are non-believers will become believers.

I decided stop here to tell Lynn I written about seeing miracles after miracles, but she said that even though it had been written once, it all needed to be written and said again.

4. By the year 2027 they will be another destruction, and it be caused by a man and will spread chaos everywhere. On that day, no one will see color anymore; instead they will see unity and will feel love toward each other. Understand humans are not animals who kill another; instead it is the job of humans to help each other.
5. Now, to the joy part. Jesus Christ will appear to someone special, and people will start to believe in this special person. It will be a special needs child; he will wake up this nation and bring it to a standstill. It will be big news.
6. Now bullies will be big factor in coming years. And, here again, someone will wake the entire nation. Those bullies will have their picture taken, and everyone will know their faces.

This is the only way that bullies will start to vanish. Some will be taken to jail. This prediction is a hard one because some of the bullies will be very young

7. This prediction is a big one: the money to the IRS will be stopped by a president.
8. Because too many people are failing to help the poor, the middle class will no longer be middle class. The middle class will become poor itself.
9. Just remember those rich people whose hiding behind curtain. The curtain will start to fall, revealing a lot of scandals to sex, rape and trafficking. It will be impossible to hide behind the curtain any more.
10. One movie star that be hit hard, not for rape, but for hatred of Blacks and Jewish.
11. Television networks will be involved in a scandal, because they produce programs that have no nice words to say about anyone, not even innocent children.
12. You need to be careful about what children see and hear. It can spell trouble for older people in the future.

My thoughts

I have to say wow, Lynn these are amazing predictions. I don't have anything to add, except one thing concerning what she had to say about the IRS. I wonder what president will stop it and why?

Now, bullies are getting out of hand, and I hope they will stop. God Bless them.

I will now let the last spirit guide Theresa tell me something.

Spirit Guide Theresa

I am here to give a lot of surprises and a testimonial to Jennie's books. Jennie has a lot of work to do and a lot of healing to impart to God's children.

1. About 99% of human race will fail to see the biggest miracle of all until 2020, and this miracle will be performed by a child.

2. Now with that being said, I will surprise the people on this earth who follows rules and regulations throughout your entire life.

3. Even though so many Earth people falling into despair, let me explain. Some presidents come to change the world; some will wake up the world to love each another by slowing hate for others.

4. There will be one president who will stop a lot of people's heartache and help bring the nation together again.

5. There will be another female president, and she will stand for love and kindness for the nation. No one will see hate that year that she is elected, and she will change history.

6. There will be another black president, and this time he, will suffer not because this person is a black president but because war break out and a lot of solders will lose their lives'. It will be the worst war in history, **so please pray**. I am Theresa have been angel, and all I see is hurt from all nationality around the world, not just one nationality everybody will be hurt by this war.

7. Islamic people will stop warring and begin the fight for peace. A vision someone sees will wake them all up. This will happen by 2028 and 2029.

8. The nation will notice a big change in weather. Severe heat will hit places for a year straight. No one will be happy, especially when it becomes cold where it never has been cold before. The weather will improve but for one entire year people will wonder if the world coming to an end. **(The answer is NO.)**

9. One president will need to step down because money is missing. This will be a big development because he is well liked by the people. Not everyone will see the truth until the cameras show it.

Now the following predictions are new to jennie and Jennie is writing it for the first time.

1. In 2018 a miracle will happen to kids close to the end of the year. No one will know until the following years that it has happened. It will be a big strange story told by children. The problem will be that the boy and girl captured evidence on camera of alien. Showing evidence to the world that Alien are real.

2. We need to be very prepared for this one. By 2029, a president will get shot but by his own gun. No one will know why he had a gun with him. The truth will be a scandal for the United State. The world will find out he used a lady without consent and she had a baby. The president won't be happy not because the world found out he has a baby but the way he handles everything.

3. Now by 2035 baby been born with HIV will be miraculously cured, and no one will know how.

4. By 2037 a president will appoint a Hispanic to be the first Latino vice president.

5. Mexico will become part of United States of America, and the wall will no longer dived America from Mexicans. This will end the deportation of Mexicans from the United States.

6. People will unite around the scandal of school shootings. This will continue for six to seven more years. until kids them-selves get tired of bulling, and that will change everything.

7. A big super star loved by so many will get murdered, and no one will understand why.

8. Earthquakes at levels of 7.10 to 10.20 will hit the biggest will be 15 point 20 and will hit the Untied States by the year 2099.

9. The cost of life will be so high that the rich people be hit with a law-suit for not preventing the homeless from freezing to death. This will happen by the year 2029 and 2030.

10. Super markets will be in a scandal. No one will be able to go on a diet not even the middle class. No one will be able to afford diet food. The world needs to change life will get hard. because the cost of food will be so high. People will go hungry and it will be a joke to the rich people. This will happen in the United Stated by the year 2030.

11. People will need to bring back rent control because the middle class will have become poor.

12. Wall Street will hit rock bottom, and the nation will see skyrocketing poverty.

13. Stores will be closing by 2060 no one will have money to buy anything.

14. People will see new light around the world no one will understand where is coming from or why is so bright. Well I let you all think about it.

My thoughts

I really can't think of anything to say after hearing Theresa' predictions. I am shock by one prediction that stands out to me: the prediction about alien. I don't know why, but it is amazing, to know that after so many TV shows about alien they may be real. I believe there is something out there that we have not seen yet. Well I guess I leave you all thinking about this. Some of you may be thinking. What is the connection between my prediction and making the world a better place? All I can say is that prove that God, not any of us is in charge, and that God ultimately, is spite of suffering and strife, will make the world a better place.

Finally, I just want you all to know if any of you is hurting inside, I am sending healing at this very moment to you as you reading this. Feel the energy filling your heart. You are not alone. You have people who care about you, even though you might not think so. Remember, reach out and talk to Jesus Christ he will take care of your sorrow.
GOD BLESS THANK YOU TO ALL MY READERS MAY ALL YOUR STRUGGLES BECOME SUCCESSES.
FINAL I WANT TO THANK MY EDITOR SHEILA
GOD BLESS YOU IN YOUR OWN JOURNEY.